Pecanartist

C.J. Krakeel

"Pecans are not cheap, my hons. In fact, in the south, the street value of shelled pecans just before holiday baking season is roughly that of crack cocaine. It is almost impossible to make a decent crack cocaine tassie, I am told." - Celia Rivenbark

"When you are describing a shape, or sound, or tint, don't state the matter plainly, but put it in a hint. And learn to look at all things with a sort of mental squint."
- Lewis Carroll

Contents

Ramblings

Olfaction

Human beings can detect over a
trillion distinct scents. I press on
the gas as night roars to life in front
of us. 'Smells Like Teen Spirit' can
only be played loud! "TURN IT UP!" you
yell. The speakers pour out the sounds,
vibrating the hairs in my nose. The
stench of whiskey and cigarettes soak
the clothes we wear, a rich oak mixed
with the addictive aura of burning
tobacco. Our t-shirts and denim jeans
now smell as stagnant as the barflies
that line up each night. You were the
only light in that staunch dive; you
drew eyes leaning over the pool table
to take your shot. You didn't notice
the back of your cue sending a glass of
Jägermeister crashing to the floor. The
smell of licorice and bad decisions
punch the bartender in the face as he
mops up your spill. I can't believe
they kicked us out. It's funny how a
smell can trigger a memory and like an
Uzi, snapshots of images now flood my
head. She loved Jägermeister. She was
much younger than you, a Hippie chick
but not the stinky type. She showered
with natural soap. Imagine pine mixed
with dirt and menthol. I like your
smell better. You are more of an
Herbal-Essences-floral-shampoo type of
girl. Your hair bounces as you move to

the music. Sitting in my front seat you
almost stop time, but we're practically
there. As we go around the bend, I can
see the giant oak tree in the distance.
You can never really ready yourself for
an impact like this. I still flinch
right before. Things are in order
though. I have a new driver's license,
new name, and a new leather wallet that
smells so good you could almost mistake
it for an old saddle being buckled up
for one last ride. I check your seat
belt. It's buckled, but I know that
will fail. I've tested it. Over and
over. The bouquet of blood and fuel
that will fill this car will be pungent
even to the most seasoned first
responders. I press on the gas and look
at you one last time as the night comes
to an abrupt stop. The windshield
shatters on impact. Time stands still.
The funk of the airbags is thick and
smoky as they deploy. Yours fails. The
bark of the tree oozes green radiator
fluid - such a sweet smell - sweet
enough to make your teeth hurt. The
song fades, "With the lights out, it's
less dangerous." I sit a few feet away
and enjoy my mess. My nostrils now
finally full of that familiar
fragrance. Human beings can detect over
a trillion distinct scents.

3

Laura Jane Grace

The show Cutthroat Kitchen with Chef
Alton Brown has always intrigued me,
but I'm not particularly fond of my
Adam's apple so I bought a Kitchen Aid
mixer with a meat grinder attachment.
Now I feel a whole lot better about
myself, and there's ground sausage in
the fridge if you're hungry.

Mourning Shift

"What are 'steak bites?'" He didn't
realize he was speaking out loud.

"Nah… you don't want that! We have a
new chef; he's in charge of the menu,"
she replies. She has flair - little
pins on her green work shirt. One's a
hamburger, and there are a few ice
cream cones and one that says "Sassy
Server."

We are welcomed into their version of
living rooms… for an evening, or a
moment, or a day. Beer taps and hard
bar stools. The smell of old fryer
grease.

"Are we going to eat here?" his eyes
watering as he looks towards the brown
liquor on the shelf.

His wife appears younger than him. Like
she's around sixty but a rough sixty. A
one-woman-army. "I'm just the driver."
She rolls her eyes as she speaks.

His mom passed the day prior. They're
in town for his granddaughter's dance
recital. New Hampshire by way of New
York and now Illinois.

We talk about Wrigley field as we watch
them. It's the off-season.

Like a river without rocks or waves, their conversation seems scripted.

By the end of the night, ten to twelve long-neck bottles are collected at the end of the bar in front of him.

"Which way to the interstate?" the woman asks the waitress.

"They need to fix our potholes. Exits are hard here, but the on-ramps are even worse." Her description of the road mirrors her weathered face. "Go out and take a left, and you're on it!" She notices her ice cream pin on the floor and picks it up as the door closes behind the couple. She stares at the zero written in the tip line.

Maybe she'll quit tonight.

Thirteen

The buttons on the face of my phone have stopped working, but it's not a mechanical malfunction. I like to think I willed them dormant with the combustibility I feel expanding in my chest from just walking into this goddamned place. She works here. She's not my mom anymore. I stand alone, back turned to them. They think I'm staring at the floor not thinking. I'm really thinking about my shoes and how they do nothing but walk all over things repeatedly. I ignore my dad to make him feel like something's wrong. My sister's smiling and talking, my brother waves goodbye to my not-mom. I don't watch as they walk out the door. "Text me when you know what time your dance recital is," Dad says. I stay silent. I've seen movies. Disney un-fucking-real-divorced-and-re-married-happiness. Fuck. I've got real problems. I'm thirteen. I'm going through changes. Alone. I won't discover self-mutilation for another year and then hard liquor not until a few years after that. If someone would put a pencil in my hand, I'd re-write fucking history. I'd write myself into this very story and only make a few grammatical mistakes.

Walking With William Styron

Souls press against the golden sea like
grain

As my cold feet step across this vast
wavy field

Eyes see the rusting of ancient farm
equipment

Tools that now even the years have
forgotten

The subtle grey water is slick and has
been for months

But the clear ice on the surface gives
it that

Ever-present feeling that the real cold
is yet to come

December is tough in this farmer's
calendar

A month that rolls his age over with
every passing

He takes the bottle of pills from his
pocket

Opening his weathered hand that has
turned this field over and over

Time and time again

And dumps ten or twelve tablets into
his palm

And like all the days before this one

He puts them to his mouth taking only
one from the bunch

Using his tongue and sticky saliva to
lift it up

He funnels the rest back into the brown
bottle

And writes, "Prozac twenty milligrams,
day two hundred and ten"

On the inner cover of his notebook

Two red and gold encrusted pheasants
sail from the wet grass

And startle this old bird dog bringing
us both back to reality

One can get lost when walking with a
poet

He opens his notebook with the words
"Darkness Visible"

Written on the cover over and over

And scribbles a few more lines

        Primo Levi, Vincent Van Gogh,
Virginia Woolf

Looking down at me, he closes it once
again

"Let's go pup, it's getting dark and
supper's on the stove"

He says with sort of a mystical nod of
the head

As if to not only acknowledge
depression but somehow cherish it

Such are things I cannot comprehend,
but

Nonetheless I follow him home like the
many times before

I Guess This Is Growing Up

I used to get excited about punk rock
shows

Now I get excited about sunny days

And the bank teller's new haircut

Makes me feel like we could work

Martin

     In the dim lit corners of his
second favorite bar, soft whispers echo
down from dirty worn walls to the stool
where Martin sits with his demons.
Five-hundred-dollar pool balls normally
sound crisp when hit with a solid
stroke but are dull to Martin's ears.
Their clattering rhythm isn't the
distraction it used to be. He chases
solace in glasses of black liquid. Each
sip a fleeting moment of numb. The cues
were all there, but no one noticed that
his reflection seemed distorted in the
polished spheres. His cue slips from
his fingers, yellow now from years of
smoke. Cylindrical wood hits the
concrete floor, a reverberating slap,
loud, like a gunshot. The room falls
quiet. His soul now forlorn. No more
clinking of glasses or the soft scrape
of chalk against a leather tip. Now
only memories linger in the haze, and
Martin's last game ends with a missed
eight-ball hanging in the pocket.

    For Martin Hall 1979-2024

The Reason I Ran

Through the diamond-shaped window of
our mobile home, I see her sitting at
the kitchen table with a Plan-B box
torn to pieces and a lukewarm Snapple.
An unlikely meal for a Tuesday night.
The gun is a Baretta 9mm. It's laying
on the table slightly off to the side
but well within reach.

Love

The monotony

        is in the bed where we sleep. It's
the weekly changing of the sheets. It's
feed the dog and pick up the cat food.
It's you sweep the floors and I'll do
the dishes. It's five A.M. again and
it's your alarm going off. I just went
to fucking bed! It's feeling tired and
content. I can't think of a single
thing worse than being content. That's
a lie. It's not winning a billion
dollars.   Is this what they mean by
mid-life crisis?! It's the gas mileage
your car gets and how that makes you
happily sad. It's the same scrubs every
day. Same scrubs, different color, but
still not red. If they were red, You.
Just. Might. Slit. Your. Wrists! That
way no one would notice the blood. It's
the grass in the yard growing faster
and faster and the heat of the summer
endlessly hot and hotter. It's your
boss and the hypocritical shit-people
you work with. It's four A.M. and why
the fuck is the dog up again. It's an
ant in the kitchen. It's ten thousand
GOD DAMN ANTS in the fucking kitchen.
It's feeling sick to your stomach as if
your body's warning you. It's a
constant job just to keep the monotony
at bay. It takes cannon ball blasts

fired daily from your middle-class pirate ship. It takes constant punching and kicking and screaming at the top of your lungs, contempt, out of breath just to keep breathing. But it's also me and it's also you! It's a kiss and a hug in the kitchen. It's a much-needed beach trip coming up. It's Lang Jewelers in San Francisco. It's that time in Buffalo by the RiverWorks when I took that photo of you. It's our confused faces as we walked out of that little white church smiling, half-laughing while trying not to cry. It's that concert in Lagrange, Georgia and him playing our song. It's Asheville, North Carolina and you in that coin-operated car. Your smile could stop the world. It's that creepy bunker we explored in Tybee Island. It's you behind the wheel of a two-door Jeep. I hid tears as we drove through the mountains in Colorado when my grandmother died. It's almost Halloween and almost time to decorate. It's the lake. It's Las Vegas. It's New York. It's Macon and Savannah. It's our home address. It's a new deck on your old house. It's your mom and dad. It's my mom and dad. It's Pine Mountain Animal Reserve and how you talked to the animals like they were people. But for

all intents and purposes, fuck emus.
It's a game of pool, just you and me at
one A.M., in our house. The house we
built. Together. It's love and it's me
and it's you and it's us.

"The purity of the road,

the white line in the middle of the highway unrolled and hugged our left front tire as if glued to our groove." You shut your door before I did, although I've been down this road before. I took the turn too fast. Not like this. I remember lying in a semi-awake state of pain and euphoria, just out of surgery in every relationship, plugged into a constant drip of fake happiness and a smile cut clear across my face. I have no idea how it got there; I just knew it shouldn't be there. I repeated this, over and over, not beating but obliterating that old dead horse. That smile finally force-faded. "The definition of insanity is doing the same thing and expecting a different outcome."

"The purity of the road, the white line in the middle of the highway unrolled and hugged our left front tire as if glued to our groove." Tires squeal and my mind races as your fingers make the same sleepy motion brushing back and forth against my arm. The two of us in one seat, driver, passenger, who cares! There are no review mirrors here, just an empty road disappearing behind us. Foot on the gas, we barrel down the road at a snail's pace stopping to check on each other at every honky-tonk

and filling station from here to
wherever, knowing that from the moment
this engine roared to life this trip
would be different.

Standing in the back

      I count the sound-proofing tiles
on the ceiling of The Masquerade while
I hold the bottom of my now-warm beer
can above my head, emptying the liquid
into my mouth. My wife looks at TikTok
and has come to the conclusion that I
have F.O.M.O. She doesn't know the
band. I sing along to the only two
songs I know and think that maybe the
eighty-dollar tickets and sixteen-
dollar beers weren't worth it. We leave
early, my ears ringing from the too-
loud-nineties-punk-rock and make our
way to a cookie shop that stays open
until 2:00am. The cookies are perfectly
warm, and hers looks better than mine.
I tell her that her diagnosis of me is
partially correct as I lean over the
center console and take a big bite of
her cookie. Crumbs fall from my lips,
and she presses on the gas.

Intimacy

It is skin and waking up hung-over to a
lemon lime Gatorade and two Tylenol.
It's volcanic passion complete with
burning lava enough to crush a thousand
Pompeii. It's baseball but not major
league. It's a cold beer after working
in the sun, son of the man next to you.
It's the sound of a bobcat in the
woods. It's a word in a dictionary you
wish you knew. It's a longing for the
beauty of untouched snow drifts long
after obtaining them. It's the moment
your eyes cease to be cameras and
become the stage. It is glass so clean
it's invisible as you walk into it face
first, hands by your side, fully aware
that your unaware.

Pets

Long Nights

It's 4:00 a.m. on a Tuesday and I can't
sleep from the pit-pat, tick, tick,
tick of her feet and nails on the
hardwood. Work is all I can think about
as sleep forms in the corner of my
eyes. I hear you sigh; you've got to be
up in an hour. This has become a common
theme, night after night, frustration
to anger to not knowing what to do. I
think about an old saying that goes
something like, this is having a dog,
this is what you signed up for, which
does not help at all and finally sleep
comes from pure exhaustion.

It's 4:00 a.m. on a Tuesday and I can't
sleep from the absence of the pit-pat,
and the tick, tick, tick of her feet
and how her nails used to hit the
hardwood. She is all I can think about
as tears form in the corners of my
eyes. I hear you cry; you've got to be
up in an hour. This has become a common
theme, every night since; frustration
to anger to not knowing what to do. I
think about an old saying that goes
something like, it's the quality of her
life not the quality she brings to
yours and she's in a better place now.
Neither help at all and finally sleep
comes from pure exhaustion.

It's Scout and it's me.

It's watching you climb the bed steps and remembering when you didn't need them.

You could leap right up!

It's getting cold outside; it hurts in my joints.

It's bad news from the vet's office that I already know.

It hurts everywhere.

It's a short-lived-new-found-love for salami.

It's dropping to my knees in the garage after vacuuming white hair from the car seats.

It was everywhere. You're still everywhere.

It's an old Lamb Chop toy and bounding energy that puts a smile on my face!

It's an old picture of you on my phone that years later will make me smile.

It's remembering how you took care of me when I broke my leg but also still breaking into a sprint when I see an armadillo!

It's knowing how much this is going to hurt.

It's sleeping at your feet with your arms clenched tight, tears welling up. I'm not going far.

It's hard trying to be tough all day. It's sleep that evades me.

It's car rides and Wendy's chicken nuggets and why am I getting so many?

It's dwelling on the past and a broken heart.

It's a full stomach. It's a happy heart. It's me hoping you're dwelling on the past, all of the good times!

It's holding up a paw for God to wipe my feet on the way in.

It's a new set of stairs and I plan on leaping up!

Parts of

songs I

never wrote

Peter Christopher

As I sat in his home in Statesboro
Georgia, Peter Christopher and I drank
glasses of wine and talked about
writing. "It's all just fucking music
in the end!" he yelled. The classical
overtures blaring form his Bose sound
system were horrible, but I was
entranced listening to Mozart and him
reading his favorite story from his
book Campfires of The Dead. "All
Thrive!!!" I remember the red wine
being thick like blood, and his voice
now sometimes sloshes through my mind.
"Go for the jugular!!!" -P.C.

I.

Genre-?

Verse

Well after ten times sober what's
another lift,

I've got a laundry list of demons and
half a fifth.

She used to drink with me, now I drink
alone,

I've got a bottle full of pills and a
broken phone.

Pre-Chorus

I wonder if there's something I can do
to make this right,

Empty bottle of pills, empty fifth and
another empty night.

II.

Genre- Country?

Verse

She's a gin and lemonade on a sunny day
somewhere between the deep south and
Bar Harbor Maine.

I'm a farmer's tan in a clear Ball Jar,
chain drinking beer in a truck-stop
bar.

She's fishing on a clear night and
wishing in the clouds.

She's home with the tv on and dinner on
the couch.

She's chase me around the bed and kiss
me on top of the head.

She's

III.

Genre- Punk Rock?

Verse

Whiskey and Katie

used to live inside of my mouth

and it was so much easier before she
got a dog

and put miles between her and the
south.

Before my fantasy was my fallacy

before I looked in the mirror and saw
thirty staring back at me.

IV.

Genre- Anarcho-Folk?

Verse

I'm the stale half-drunk beer
On the ledge above the urinal
I'm a pumping fist
In front of a band
That's losing popularity
I look at the police state
And scream fuck this economy
We tailor to bullshit and harbor fear
As our great nation loses popularity

Musings

Waffle House

As I sit in this booth, my mind jumps
from topic to topic. Thing to thing.
Thing to thinking. I ponder her life
and the not-so-distant death of my
father. I wonder how he will go. I
imagine however it happens, it will be
long after my mother goes. She will go
first. It will be this or that - this
cancer or that cirrhosis - and she'll
joke about either, quick to have one of
us kids bring a potted violet to give
to her nurse as she struggles to make a
sentence. My mind goes back to lost
thoughts, and every memory fills a
square in a Waffle House waffle with
syrup. Twelve years old in a van on our
way to Greenwood, South Carolina to
take care of my grandparents, Johnny
Cash sang, "I'm stuck in Folsom Prison,
and time keeps dragging on." My mother
was never stuck. She drug on. She took
care of them, unasked for, unfathomable
love. She takes another drag from her
gas-station green brand cigarette. The
hospital walls close in, and I realize
none of us are her. None of us can say
we're any better than the next. The
syrup container sticks to my napkin,
and as always, we stick to our guns,
unloaded, off the menu, what-we-think-
is-right, GUNS. It will be these guns

34

that one day pay the tab. You're an
all-star. Would you like a to-go drink?

Turning Forty

It's funny how in times like these your
mouth turns to saltwater and you're
once again fifteen years old, fighting
a scuba mask from Walmart like it's
life or death, like fuck this - it's
way too tight, the imprints on your
face seem to last for hours! Even the
waitress at Capitan Jack's makes a
comment, and your dad's rescue-dive-
team-flippers that keep sliding off
your feet because they're three sizes
too big are the only things that keep
you grounded. Without them, you would
be the next person eaten by a shark. In
two feet of ocean, you stake your
claim! Your teeth are buoys now,
keeping the waves calm until the big
boat that's really your last shot of
whiskey comes roaring by. Spewing a
rooster tail of vomit across the now-
glass-like-sea and as your mind spins
into your current choppy situation,
you're alive, you're happy, you're
happy... and holy crap, you're Forty.

Divorce

Happy people sit and wonder why
marriage ends. How can something once
so perfect fizzle like an Alka-Seltzer
tablet dropped into the last broken
glass of whiskey? How can someone so in
love look at a candle and spit on the
same fire they lit? Once roaring with
flame, now sending it's fading strength
into a smoldering wick, ugly with the
last embers, slowly burning out.

Jumping To Incorrect Conclusions

It sucks when the balls start to roll
off. The pool table's clean and
leveled. Leveled enough. Enough where
after only a few years, the balls
shouldn't be rolling off. But things
settle. Houses settle, floors settle. I
know this because the caulk I applied
to keep this relationship together is
starting to crack. It will smooth
though, when the wood swells in the
summer. It's nothing new and it's
unavoidable. How you handle the here
and now and the after is what matters.
I remember a day in the sun and my
mother in a bikini and a bunch of my
friends jumping off a bridge, and I
stood feet burning on the July blacktop
watching as they hit the cool water.

Cold Beer

I pry at the lid using all my fingers.
Wedging them between the two surfaces,
I pull and break the semi-air-tight
seal. Once open, I start by touching
the floating pieces of ice, poking them
and watching as they plunge beneath the
water and re-surface. I remove a small
piece and let the dog lick it as it
melts; it drips onto the floor and
disappears from my grasp. The dog laps
up the resulting puddle. I stare back
into the depths and insert my hand; the
water is a cold stream in a magazine at
a stale dentist's office. I move a bag
of sliced turkey. It slightly leaks its
juice into the frigid water. My wrists
pass the surface line, and I'm almost
elbow deep. I turn my head to the side
to get a little more reach. My hands
begin to go numb like they do when you
wear that one dress that's a little too
tight; my fingers scrape the bottom of
the Igloo cooler and come to a halt
against cold, cylindrical, metal,
aluminum. I drag the can up towards the
surface, and like a whale, it springs
from the depths and out into the fresh
air.

Retirement Planning

Seven big IPAs make my cheeks feel like
two tennis balls, not green with
envious fur but a bright pink. Not the
normal pink that you'd see on MTV, but
the pink that you long for when you
test lipstick on the shelf at Walmart.
You drag the soft substance across cold
dystopian metal, a metaphor for your
relationships, for what you've become.
It's funny that I only write when my
equilibrium is compromised and you are
fast asleep inches from my fingers. I
don't crave discomfort nor struggle,
but my blood alcohol level reminisces
back to a lyric that explains
everything: "Livin's better when taking
chances constantly." My fingers no
longer finger, and my mind drifts to
weird dreams. She's beside me, and
somehow, I'm beside myself. Save your
money. Put coins in a piggy bank. It
won't ease your mind. It won't ever
make a difference, but in a few months,
it might buy you a few beers.

Internationally Hungover

It's not that his body isn't tired. His
muscles now three days sore from
planting magnolias and uncomfortable
seats on long flights to places he
doesn't even want to be. It's his
addiction to whiskey, corrupted by
nuevo-cocaine-based energy drinks that
boast a five-hour label that keep his
mind slowly turning. His thoughts
mirror a slow-motion fan overhead,
rotating in the big bedroom where he
lays as the heavy light pull slaps
against the cut crystal globe. His head
spins.

Eulogies

Thank you all for coming. Thanks,
everyone, for coming. I'm glad everyone
was able to come celebrate the life-
what the fuck.

I count, out loud, using my fingers. I
try to estimate how many potential
funerals I will attend in the next
twenty years. I run out of fingers and
then toes. I need to write more. My
skin shrivels in the bath. I need to
write more. I need to write eulogies
for my own parents that I will never be
satisfied with.

I take old pictures off the walls in my
childhood home. The AC hasn't been on
in months. Finishing nails protrude
from the smoke-stained walls. The
wallpaper behind the frames is just
slightly less brown. Instead of pulling
the nails I hit them into the
sheetrock. These damn walls will need
to come down to the studs anyway.

Thank you all for coming.

On Writing

Paper compacts in my palms. It wrinkles
and becomes something less. Small
waste-basketballs of my innocence. The
smell of failure hangs in the back of
my nostrils. It breathes. It echoes. It
causes chaos. The marriage to the
marathon, to the whored-out paper,
screaming within college ruled lines.
The waste basket overflows.

You always said my writing was trash.

End.

Citations

Olfaction- Lines 48-49. "Smells Like Teen Spirit," Nirvana.

The purity of the road- Lines 1-4 and 21-24. *On the Road*, Jack Kerouac.

Retirement Planning- Lines 16-17. "Thing Of The Past," Tim Barry.

Printed 2024

For

Gremlin Growlers

The Vandals Inside Gremlin Growlers

Alan Michael Parker's vandals are
screaming, coffee is brewing.
The barista hides beneath the counter.

In the poem about vandals and breaking
the law,
A patron rests their beer on a
forgotten comma.

Beer spills. (The poem is soaked.)
The vandals cheer as they urinate in
the coffee.

They whoop like monkeys and swing
From the beer taps on the counter.

The liquid drips from the vandals'
mouths,
We all know how vandals love Abstract
Expressionism.

But their art is different today—
Alcohol and caffeine have made the
vandals crazy.

In a turn of the page, a lone vandal
escapes.
(This has never happened before. A
vandal now able

To wreak havoc on the real world. Or so
we thought.)
The vandal leaps from the page and is
met with force—

A smiling gremlin seems to growl as it
chases the vandal
Around the poem and back into the
depths of the book.

The vandal howls for his cronies, and
they all take shelter... behind a
broken sentence, fragmented and
incomplete. Their plan unraveling.

Made in the USA
Columbia, SC
25 October 2024

45052480R00038